Sis, You Are Amazing

Sis, You Are Amazing

30 Days of Encouragement

Janine Faulkner

Unless otherwise noted all scripture quotations are taken from the King James Version®.

Scripture quotations marked (NKJ) are taken from the New King James version. Copyright © 1982 by Thomas Nelson, Inc. Used by permission. All rights reserved.

Scripture quotations marked (NIV) are taken from the Holy Bible, New International Version®, NIV®. Copyright © 1973, 1978, 1984, 2011 by Biblica, Inc.™ Used by permission of Zondervan. All rights reserved worldwide. www.zondervan.com The "NIV" and "New International Version" are trademarks registered in the United States Patent and Trademark Office by Biblica, Inc.™

Printed in the United States of America

21 20 19 18 17   987654321

Author's website: www.gratefullifecreation.com

ISBN: 978-0-692-99627-0

Book/cover design: Tawanda Prince

Editor: Tawanda Prince

Published by: Grateful Life Creations

30 Days

1. Know Yourself
2. Love Yourself
3. Dream Again
4. Believe in Yourself
5. You Are Enough
6. You Are Valuable
7. You Are Beautiful
8. You are Greatness
9. You Have God's Favor
10. You Are Blessed
11. Pray
12. The Spirit of the Lord is on You
13. For He Knows the Plans He Has for You
14. Greater is He that is in You
15. You Can Do All Things through Christ
16. The Battle Is Not Yours
17. God Has Not Given You the Spirit of Fear
18. Surrender All
19. Be Still and Know
20. Your Gift Will Make Room for You
21. It's Not Too Late
22. Be Thankful
23. Celebrate
24. Let it Be Well with Your Soul
25. Let Him Restore Your Soul

A Word from the Author

Hello, and welcome to Sis, You Are AMAZING! This book is a journaling experience to help uplift you, renew your self-love and to remind you of the promises of God.

I wrote this book because I have been working hard to rediscover myself as I transition into the next phase of my life. As I watch my kids complete college and as I see my mirror image of myself changing, I realized that I needed to rediscover myself, my loves, my dreams, and my God.

Many of my friends are going through the same transitional period, and we support each other along the way. However, sometimes in those lonely, private moments, we need a quick boost of confidence or a good word to help us keep moving forward. My intentions are that this book helps you recapture your strength, beauty and confidence, so you remember, Sis, You Are AMAZING!

Much Love,

Janine Faulkner

Hey, Sis! I hope you are feeling amazing! If you are not at your best today, this book was written to remind you that you are an awesome creation! Really! Sometimes, you need to be reminded of who you are. You are a queen and should hold your head up and know that you have value.

There are times when we feel like we are on top of the world. Our hair is right, the body is tight (or trying), and we are dressed to the nines, feeling like a million bucks. We are also healthy, energized and thinking positively.

Then there are times we ask ourselves, "What is going on?" The hair will not look right, we feel unattractive, and we are just tired of everything. We feel down, and our thinking is negative and self-defeating. For some of us, we feel this way a little more often than we would like to admit.

On a daily basis, I have to work to keep a positive outlook on my life. Going to work every day, running a business and taking care of my family can be challenging. I mean challenging! Maybe I'll write a book on that too. However, things can happen in the course of a day to make it a bad day or a great day.

Let's take the next 30 days to have more great days! I want to encourage you daily to be uplifted when things get challenging. I want to elevate your spirits when you get down and help you renew your mind in those discouraging moments.

Each day and title represents an inspirational pillow that I made especially for you at GratefulLifeCreations.com. Stop there and click the Sis, You are Amazing button to order the pillow that speaks personally to you.

Follow me on this journey of self-love, seeking God and living a fuller, happier life so that you can remember, Sis, You are AMAZING!

DAY 1

KNOW YOURSELF

My dear Sis, do you really know who you are? Have you ever felt unsure of what you want for your future? It is ok! These answers change as we mature. It's important for you to discover what you love about life and explore more of that. Then you become clearer about who you are. I did that in 2014, when I sent my son off to college and began to prepare my daughter for her senior year in high school. I needed to figure out what would be my next steps. Not fullfilled by my 9-5, I needed something to nurture my soul. I began to explore jewelry. That was not it. Then drawing, that was not it, either. Then I bought a sewing machine, remembering how I enjoyed sewing a sundress with my grandmother when I was in middle school. That was it! My journey led me to sewing inspirational pillows, and now I have a growing business that I love.

Know yourself spiritually. Know yourself physically. Discover what is important to you and why you make the choices you make. Analyze your thoughts and think about your past and present, and determine what you want for your future.

SELF DISCOVERY

Write down your strengths and your weaknesses. Write down what you love. Write what you want to do in life and how you will make it happen.

_____

_____

_____

_____

_____

_____

_____

_____

_____

_____

_____

_____

_____

Soon, you will know more about what makes you happy, and you can live the life God intends for you. God created you for a reason. Sis, know you are one of a kind, and no one is better at being you than you. Lift your head and be confident in who YOU are and who YOU are becoming! Find what you love, do it more, master it, and master being YOU.

Day 2

Love Yourself

You hear it all the time. You have to love yourself! If you do not love yourself, you will not be able to love anyone else.

For many years, I never thought about loving myself. Being a wife and mother, I put all my time into my family. Throwing birthday parties, going to PTA meetings, and housekeeping consumed my days. I can not remember giving myself much time to do anything for myself and show self-love. When I saw my kids in high school going off to college, transitioning into their adult lives, I realized I needed to start transitioning too. I began to look within and develop a new lifestyle that forced me to live life to the fullest. I started doing more for myself and loving on myself by going to the doctor to address issues. I started a fitness plan, and I began buying things for myself, as I never did in the past. I also started looking at my relationships. I had to let some people go. It is not always easy to take action for a better life, but it is necessary in order for you to love yourself freely and unapologetically. You must love yourself, not in an arrogant way, but in a healthy way.

SELF DISCOVERY

How do you love yourself? The answer is different for each woman. For some, it may be connecting to God or taking a day off work. For others, it may be a regularly scheduled spa day, reading, decluttering your environment, or traveling with loving family and friends.

Define what self-love is to you and write down the actions you will take to love yourself every day. How will you love yourself today?

_____

_____

_____

_____

_____

_____

_____

_____

_____

_____

_____

_____

Do something special every day for YOURSELF.

DAY 3

DREAM AGAIN

When you were a little girl, what did you want to be when you grew up? Some of you knew right away that you wanted to be a lawyer, a doctor, or a business owner. Some of you may have dreamed of being a wife, mother of three kids, and having a home with a dog, in the suburbs. Looking back, you may not have reached your dreams.

I always dreamed of having a J-O-B, a husband, kids, and a rancher style home. God blessed me with just that. Notice I said, just that. I did not require much of God, did I? Well, Sis, I now realize that I can dream bigger dreams and I am in the process of figuring out what those dreams are. I thank God for what he has given me, but God has MORE out there to be discovered and life can be whatever you want it to be. So I am dreaming again, and I am excited about my future like the Psalm 31 woman. I am taking action, trying new things, and doing things even when I am afraid. Like writing this book!

SELF DISCOVERY

Looking back, what dreams are yet to be fullfilled?
Looking forward, what do you want for your life, now?
Write those dreams. How will you make this happen?

_____

_____

_____

_____

_____

_____

_____

_____

_____

_____

_____

_____

_____

_____

_____

_____

_____

Do not stop believing in your dreams. You still have time
to be and do what you desire.

DAY 4

BELIEVE IN YOURSELF

You cannot accomplish much if you do not believe in yourself. You ought to have something inside you to keep you going when doubt tries to take over your mind. Not only do you have to believe in yourself, but you need to believe in a higher power. For me, that is God. *"For with God, nothing shall be impossible."* *Luke 1:37* You simply have to believe that what you want to happen is possible and not doubt. Yes, it can be hard to just believe when your money is funny, your man is acting crazy or your body is breaking down. But Sis, the older I get, the more I understand that God wants us to believe in ourselves and him so he can bless us.

SELF DISCOVERY

What are some things you are believing for today? What things are you doubting? How can you change the doubts to beliefs?

_____

_____

_____

_____

_____

_____

_____

_____

_____

_____

Sis, this is one of the most important parts of the journey. Believe you can have what you want and move towards it without doubting; then you will have it. Push out the negative thoughts for something you want today and watch things open up for you. You are amazing! Believe in yourself! Believe in yourself!! Believe in YOURSELF!!!

DAY 5

YOU ARE ENOUGH

Sis, you are enough! Just as you are. God made you unique and for a purpose. Perfection does not exist. Everyone has flaws, but no one can ever be YOU. You can self-improve until you leave this earth, but there is something that sets you apart from everyone else. No one talks like you, no one has your energy, no one has your spunk, and no one loves like you do. Your eyes, your thoughts, your ways are all you! You are a combination of traits, skills, moods, talents, emotions, and intellect that does not exist in anyone else. God designed you to custom fit your life. He has a reason for creating you the way you are. Sis, you are enough!

SELF DISCOVERY

Write down your personality traits and unique gifts that make you stand out from the rest.

_____

_____

_____

_____

_____

_____

_____

_____

_____

_____

Nurture those gifts and quirks that make you unique and celebrate them. Someone out there will love you exactly the way you are. You have something in you that can possibly change the world. Do not underestimate the importance of your existence.

DAY 6

YOU ARE VALUABLE

Sometimes, people can make you discount your worth. Something may have happened in your past like being teased or violated by someone. Perhaps you have a critical parent who you can never please. You might work for a negative supervisor who refusees to acknowledge anything good about your hard work. You might be with a man that is abusive or negelectful. There may be someone else mistreating you, like a family member, associate, co-worker or neighbor.

Sis, do your best to avoid those negative people and situations. Being around negativity hurts your thought process and negative energy can make you negative too. If the negativity is at work, take frequent walks or a time-out to reduce stress. If it is your mate, you can seek outside help and give it your all until you have peace about your next step. Keep working to improve yourself, because unless they change, you will not grow and flourish constantly being around them. Surround yourself with people who love you and want the best for you. Their positivity will make you happier and even healthier.

SELF DISCOVERY

Name some people in your life that are negative. Note how you will make changes in how you handle those people.

_____

_____

_____

_____

_____

_____

_____

_____

_____

_____

_____

_____

The Bible says, "*You are more precious than rubies.*" *Proverbs 3:15*. Believe it and do not let anyone take your worth away from you, EVER!

DAY 7

YOU ARE BEAUTIFUL

I used to hate my nose. I thought it was too wide and too flat. I was teased for being boney and flat chested. I rarely felt beautiful. I did not see my true beauty until after having my children. I realized the miracles my body was blessed to experience. I also put on weight and finally got my curves, some unwanted dimples, and some stretch marks. So what! This is me, and I decided I am beautiful just as I am, with all my flaws and imperfections. Things constantly change as I age, even with a fitness regimen, but I still know I am beautiful, and so should you!

Look in the mirror and love what you see because it is who God made you to be. Dark, light, big, small, tall, short, knock-kneed, real hair, or a weave, you are beautiful. Take care of the precious gift that is you, and know you are beautiful, no matter what. Don't forget, media images are often photoshopped and not real. Stop comparing yourself. Beauty is in the eye of the beholder. You are someone's dream, so don't mess yourself up being something you are not.

SELF DISCOVERY

Write a list of what you do not like about yourself that cannot be changed. Now, write "I love my" in front of each one.

_____

_____

_____

_____

_____

_____

_____

_____

_____

_____

_____

_____

_____

Now turn these statements into personal affirmations. Say these every day until you believe them.

DAY 8

YOU ARE GREATNESS

Sis, you are GREAT! Sis, you are AWESOME! Sis, you are AMAZING!

SELF DISCOVERY

Write a list of 15 things that make you AMAZING. Look at this list when you feel doubt trying to get in your spirit. Attack doubt with your greatness.

_____

_____

_____

_____

_____

_____

_____

_____

_____

_____

_____

_____

_____

_____

Sis, know you are worthy and walk in your greatness!

DAY 9

YOU HAVE GOD'S FAVOR

"Do not let kindness and truth leave you; bind them around your neck, write them on the tablet of your heart. So you will find favor and success in the sight of God and man." Proverbs 3:3-4

Have you ever wondered how a person gains favor in their life? This scripture answers that question. Being kind and being truthful is the key to favor. It is as simple as that. Find ways to be kind to people. Start with a kind smile or a kind word.

Think of some people that you know who need some kindness in their lives. The scripture instructs you to, "Bind kindness and truth around your neck and write them on the table of your heart." This shows how important these are for you to receive favor.

The Bible also says, *"Speak the truth in love"* *Eph 4:15*. In addition, his love, kindness and truth yield God's favor. The more you practice these principles, the more favor you will have in your life.

SELF DISCOVERY

Write down what you will do to brighten the day of someone else. What action will you take immediately?

_____

_____

_____

_____

_____

_____

_____

_____

_____

_____

_____

_____

_____

_____

_____

_____

_____

When you think of others, God gives you Favor.

DAY 10

YOU ARE BLESSED

Sometimes, things can look so bad that we can not see the good. Just look around and count your blessings. Your health, your family, and the roof over your head. You are blessed. You have transportation, and you became well when you were sick. You are blessed. You woke up this morning, and you made it through yesterday when you didn't think you would. You are blessed.

You must cast your cares on him. It is hard not to worry when bad things happen in your life, but you know that you must give your problems to God and leave them with him. What does that mean? That means do not stress over the things that you cannot change but to give them to God for him to work out and trust that he will. No matter if your issues revolve around money, health, family or relationships, you are at your best when you are not carrying those extra weights around. He wants the best for you. Sis, you are BLESSED!

SELF DISCOVERY

What weights do you have to put down and give to God? Write down the blessings that surround you right now.

_____

_____

_____

_____

_____

_____

_____

_____

_____

_____

_____

_____

_____

Sis, you are surrounded by blessings every day. Take notice and be thankful.

DAY 11

PRAY

In order to cast your cares on God, you must pray. Prayer is simply talking to God. Sis, you need to talk to God every day as much as possible. God loves you and wants to help you along your journey. When you seek him, he can help you get through when times get rough. Just talk to him. Talk to him in the car, on the bus, in the bathroom, while taking a walk, while waiting for an appointment, and before you go to sleep. If you are in a situation where you cannot speak aloud, then talk to him in your spirit. Also Sis, do not just talk to God when things are going bad but talk to him when things are going well. Exalt him, thank him, and praise him for the great things you are experiencing. He will hear you and bless your situation.

Acknowledge his power, thank him for his goodness, and ask him for what you need. He will supply!

SELF DISCOVERY

How can you add more prayer to your daily walk? Write
a short prayer to God about your concerns.

_____

_____

_____

_____

_____

_____

_____

_____

_____

_____

_____

_____

_____

_____

_____

_____

_____

_____

Sis, God is amazing and prayer opens the door for him
to bless you.

DAY 12

THE SPIRIT OF THE LORD IS ON YOU-LUKE 4:18

Sis, you have an anointing on your life. Anointing is similar to purpose. As you learn who you are, how to love yourself, and how to walk in your purpose, you are becoming more useful to God. God will entrust you with more responsibility that benefits you and others. You cannot let that go to waste. Just think, you did not get hit by that car, you were healed, your bills were paid anyway, you may have been raised in a mess, but you are now a miracle. God has his hand on you and wants your life to glorify him.

"But the anointing which you have received from Him abides in you, and you do not need that anyone teach you; but as the same anointing teaches you concerning all things, and is true, and is not a lie, and just as it has taught you, you will abide in Him." 1 John 2:27(NKJV)

You can use your anointing to do great things with confidence that God is with you! If you do not know what to do with your anointing, seek God for answers. When you spend time in his presence he will speak to your heart about your anointing. He has a special purpose for your gifts to further advance his kingdom.

SELF DISCOVERY

Write down some things that make it evident that the Spirit of the Lord is on you.

_____
_____
_____
_____
_____
_____
_____
_____
_____
_____
_____
_____
_____
_____
_____
_____
_____
_____
_____

Your anointing is most powerful when you know you are anointed and you walk in it. Walk in God's glory!

DAY 13

FOR HE KNOWS THE PLANS HE HAS FOR YOU-*JEREMIAH 29:11*

My anointed sister, you can rest in the confidence that God knows the plans that he has for you. That means you have a bright and promising future. As you grow, you can wake up every day knowing that God has your back. His plans for you include good health, love, prosperity, and an abundant life. It is already yours even though sometimes life's circumstances may appear otherwise. Just expect him to unveil your future every day in a way that will blow your mind.

What God does in your life is measured by your faith. He knows what you need, so believe he will provide. Yes, you will have some trouble, but God is bigger than any trouble now and in our future. Sis, his plans for you are amazing!

SELF DISCOVERY

Name some things in your life that God changed for the better.

_____

_____

_____

_____

_____

_____

_____

_____

_____

_____

_____

_____

_____

_____

_____

_____

_____

Remember, *"All things work together for the good of them who love the Lord and are called according to his purpose."* Romans 8:28.

DAY 14

GREATER IS HE THAT IS IN YOU

I JOHN 4:4

When troubles come, and when life gets out of hand, God is more powerful than any problems or any individual that comes in your path. When events overwhelm you and people try to consume you, lean on God and know that he will fix it.

God is more than a common man. He is the creator of the universe. Nothing is too large or small for him to work out. Sis, you are amazing because the amazing God who dwells inside of you created you in his AMAZING image.

SELF DISCOVERY

Make a list of 3-5 of your current problems. Write
"GIVEN TO GOD" in all caps next to each problem.

_____

_____

_____

_____

_____

_____

_____

_____

_____

_____

_____

_____

Remind yourself that God can do anything but fail.
Refer to this list if you begin to doubt, and trust that
God will supply all your needs.

DAY 15

YOU CAN DO ALL THINGS
THROUGH CHRIST *PHILIPPIANS 4:13*

God allows you to sleep at night and opens your eyes every morning to a new day. God allows you to step out of your bed, get dressed, eat, and start your day, even when you do not feel like it. God gives you the strengh to do whatever you need to do each day, so you can surely do all things through him. He blesses you to breathe without you even thinking about it, so you can do anything you want, need, or have to do.

Speak life and feed your faith, not your lack. Change your negative thinking and speaking to positivity. Change your circle if you have to. Place yourself amongst people who are stronger than you who will push or pull you forward. Affirm yourself daily with things you need to believe about yourself. Yes, you can!

SELF DISCOVERY

Write down the things that you are confident about.

_____

_____

_____

_____

_____

_____

_____

_____

_____

_____

_____

_____

_____

_____

_____

_____

Be confident in the new you that you are becoming, get over your fears and get busy. Sis, you CAN!

DAY 16

THE BATTLE IS NOT YOURS

2 CHRONICLES 20:15

Sis, whatever you might be going through, you already have the victory. When Jesus died on the cross, then rose up on the third day, he won and so did you.

Jesus took your place and took the stripes and pain. He suffered for your shortcomings and he was hung up for your hang ups. Although there may be times when you get some cuts and bruises from a fight, you have the victory in Jesus. Whether the battle is at your job, home, school, ministry or relationships, it is already won. It is wonderful to know that even though he has equipped you to win some small fights, ultimately he will fight and win the battle for you. Fight with prayer, praise and the word and know you are victorious.

SELF DISCOVERY

Write down the battles you will let God fight for you.

_____

_____

_____

_____

_____

_____

_____

_____

_____

_____

_____

_____

_____

_____

_____

_____

_____

_____

_____

Have faith for those "fiery darts", and always pray expecting to be victorious.

Day 17

GOD HAS NOT GIVEN YOU THE SPIRIT OF FEAR   *2 TIMOTHY 1:7*

Sis, you do not have to be afraid. If you are dealing with issues at work, with your man, family, business or health, you do not have to be afraid. God has a way of working things out. He has a way of opening up doors that you did not know existed.

Yes, there are evil forces out there that want to take away your bright future. When you give in to that, fear wins. You have to speak something different and powerful to your situation. You have to go back to believing and standing on God's word. God has given you power, love, and a sound mind. These are the tools you need to use to overcome fear.

SELF DISCOVERY

Isaiah 35:4-"Say to those with fearful hearts 'Be strong, do not fear; your God will come…" (NIV)

John 14:27-"Peace I leave with you; my peace I give you. I do not give to you as the world gives. Do not let your hearts be troubled and do not be afraid." (NIV)

Matthew 6:34-"Do not worry about tomorrow. Each day has enough trouble of its own." (NIV)

Joshua 1:9-"Have I not commanded you? Be strong and courageous. Do not be afraid; do not be discouraged, for the Lord your God will be with you wherever you go." (NIV)

Psalm 23:4-"Even though I walk through the darkest valley, I will fear no evil. For you are with me; your rod and your staff they comfort me." (NIV)

Romans 8:38-39- "For I am convinced that neither death nor life, neither angels nor demons, neither the present nor the future, nor any powers, neither height nor depth, nor anything else in all creation, will be able to separate us from the love of God that is in Christ Jesus our Lord." (NIV)

List four ways you overcame fear this week.

_____

_____

_____

_____

_____

_____

_____

_____

_____

_____

_____

_____

_____

_____

_____

_____

_____

Apply the principles of these scriptures and go for what is yours!

DAY 18

SURRENDER ALL

Sometimes, you have things inside of you that you have not given to God. There are things from your past that you are still holding on to. There are grudges that you are holding against people which keep you trapped in unforgiveness. There are failures and regrets that you have experienced that keep you in bondage. These things can block your blessings and cause you to not be as close to God as you should be.

When you hold on to bad habits and beliefs it can stunt your growth. In order to surrender, you need to face your issues, determine your truths, and be honest with God. Verbalizing your truth to God helps you to wipe the slate clean and become free. Just tell God, "Here it is, Lord. I have dealt with this long enough. Please take this now." When you give God your mess for him to fix, then you surrender all.

SELF DISCOVERY

Write down five things that are blocking your blessings
that you will surrender to God.

_____

_____

_____

_____

_____

_____

_____

_____

_____

_____

_____

_____

_____

_____

_____

The only way to truly free yourself is to surrender all
things. Big and small he wants them all.

DAY 19

BE STILL AND KNOW-*PSALM 46-10*

Life is busy. There are so many things to do and so many instructions to follow in order to improve your life. Sometimes, the stress of all the expectations and goals can be overwhelming. When you have done all you can do and when you are feeling overloaded, be still.

It is amazing what you will discover when you take a few moments to be still. Take some time to be quiet with God. Listen to him in your heart. He will give you clarity in the confusion. He will give you a message in the midst of the mess. There is a blessing in the stillness, so just be still...

SELF DISCOVERY

Take one minute of quiet time right now and listen to God's voice. What do you hear in your heart?

_____

_____

_____

_____

_____

_____

_____

_____

_____

_____

_____

Before bed, think of him for revelation as you sleep. Listen! His voice is positive and loving. The negative voices are not of him. Push those thoughts out and hear the positive. He will give you peace within. Seek him!

DAY 20

YOUR GIFT WILL MAKE ROOM FOR YOU-*PROVERBS 18:16*

Some of your financial problems can be solved by stepping out and using your gifts. God has given you gifts and talents to help you provide for you and your family. He has also given you gifts to bless others and to use for his glory. Stepping out with my sewing and hand crafting pillows, to provide inspiration to others, has blessed my spirit to the core. It has opened up so many parts of me that I did not even know I had. Making my pillows gives me life and helps me to explore and enjoy new opportunities. It also helps me to bless others. Even though I am afraid sometimes, I have to leave the comfort zone and evolve. Even though I sometimes question my products' relevance, I go out to vending opportunities anyway. I see that many people love my pillows and buy them for personal encouragement and for gifts.

Use your gifts and you will grow. Your gifts are for you to give to the world. People are out there waiting for what you have to offer. Your gifts will surely make room for you and Sis, you will be amazed how you will bless others.

SELF DISCOVERY

What are your gifts and talents? What gives you life?
How can you be a blessing with your your gifts?

_____

_____

_____

_____

_____

_____

_____

_____

_____

_____

What gives you life might just save someone else's life.
Do it for yourself. Do it for others. Do it for God.

DAY 21

IT'S NOT TOO LATE

Sis, it is never too late to start dreaming. Sometimes your dreams of the past were never attained. You have to renew those dreams or create new dreams. Some of the dreams you never accomplished can still happen if you set your mind to do it. You can go back to school, start a business or ministry, get married, birth or "mother" a child, travel, or support a passionate cause. Perhaps you want to lose weight, write a book, buy your dream home or become Miss America, whatever you want to do, you can still have all you desire. The sky is the limit!

Some dreams take more to accomplish than others. See what you have to do to reach your goal and make a plan. Network and get a mentor or a coach. You will be surprised at who you will connect with to accomplish your dreams. God strategically places people in your life to be a blessing to you. Be open to new options and God will give you the desires of your heart.

SELF DISCOVERY

Write a bucket list of ten things you want to accomplish.

_____

_____

_____

_____

_____

_____

_____

_____

_____

_____

_____

_____

_____

_____

_____

_____

_____

_____

Set a plan to accomplish these things. Do not let your dreams and goals die! Sis, it's not too late to begin...or begin again.

DAY 22

BE THANKFUL

Live each day with gratitude. Have a grateful heart. If today does not go so well, try again tomorrow. Lift your head up. Think positive thoughts.

You have a lot to be thankful for. You cannot ever forget that there is always something to thank God for. Sometimes you do not only need to be thankful for what you have but for what you do not have. Just think about how many trials you did not have to face alone or at all. God has given you a life to be grateful for and there are many who would love to trade places with you. Things for me truly changed when I focused on being grateful. When you are thankful for the blessings that you already have, God will bless you with even more.

SELF DISCOVERY

Read the blessings you wrote on Day 10. Add five more
to the list.

_____

_____

_____

_____

_____

_____

_____

_____

_____

_____

It feels great when someone expresses thanks to you, so
do that for God!

Day 23

Celebrate

Sis, celebrate yourself, celebrate life, and celebrate what is going well. Celebrate when you get a good grade, celebrate when you accomplish something at work, and celebrate when you can open the door to a bright and sunny day. Celebrate how you have evolved, how you overcame obstacles, and how you are living victoriously. Celebrate the increase in your faith walk. Celebrate how you have learned to love, forgive and accept yourself and others.

Celebration is important. You need to make a big deal out of your accomplishments because they take a lot of work. Celebration gives you the boost you need to uplift your mood and make you feel like doing even more. Celebration time gives you an opportunity to reward yourself, acknowledge your accomplishments and share with those who support you. So praise God and CELEBRATE!

SELF DISCOVERY

What do you need to celebrate today? How will you celebrate?

_____
_____
_____
_____
_____
_____
_____
_____
_____
_____

CELEBRATE...Sis, you are AMAZING!

Day 24

Let it be Well with Your Soul

You are not going to like everything that happens in your life. Some of the things you prayed not to happen, did. Some things you hope will happen, will not. You may have really been counting on something like a business deal or a promotion, a job offer after acing an interview, etc., but that thing just did not happen. It is at these times you need to accept what God allows and let it be well with your soul. Also, you may need to release some people and expectations. After all, God knows best, right? Of course he does. You just have to get out of your feelings sometimes, and just let God be God.

You have been given life, so you need to enjoy it. God gave you life to live and experience abundance on this side, not to wait until you get to heaven. Do not get hung up on what is not God's best for you. If you find that you are stuck, get help from a pastor, mental health professional, life coach or trusted friend.

It helps to take time to find that place of balance and inner peace. Set the atmoshere by surrounding yourself with things that make you feel good. Candles, water fountains, aromatherapy, scented oils, mood lighting, music and of course, Grateful Life Creations pillows. When you surround yourself with these things, it feeds your soul. Make peace with where you are in life, then take steps to improve it, and then it will be well with your soul.

SELF DISCOVERY

Write down a list of what is not well with your soul.
Reread the list and cross out each item and write next
to it, **IT IS WELL!**

_____

_____

_____

_____

_____

_____

_____

_____

_____

_____

_____

_____

_____

_____

Light a scented candle if you have one. Take in the smell
and the illumination of the light in your room and enjoy
it. Say a prayer of peacefull release and acceptance.

DAY 25

LET HIM RESTORE YOUR SOUL
PSALM 23:3

God knows just what you need. He will restore your soul when you allow him to do so. When it is well with your soul, let God work, and rest in him knowing he has you in the palm of his hand. He can restore your soul and renew your way of thinking. It can take time, but when you let go, it feels so good to know God will fill your needs with what he knows is best for you.

Also, you need physical things such as water, healthy food, rest, vacation, massage, music, hobbies, fellowship and creative outlets to help restore the mind, body and soul. Enjoy more of these things. Spend time with people who help ignite your faith, not hinder it. Your soul's restoration requires balance of the physical, mental and spiritual. You must seek God first to find complete restoration.

SELF DISCOVERY

What is preventing your soul from being restored? List
five specific things you can do to restore your soul.

_____

_____

_____

_____

_____

_____

_____

_____

_____

_____

_____

_____

_____

_____

Restoration of the soul is important, so make it a daily
practice as often as possible.

DAY 26

TRUST GOD

Trusting God is the key that unlocks the door to inner peace. When you trust God, then you can truly say, "It is well with my soul," and let him restore your soul as only he can. Trusting God means knowing that no matter how it may look, it will be alright. You must remind yourself that God's promises do exist.

When you trust God, you are in better shape for your future. To truly be at peace you must trust God; not mama, not sister, not Boo, but GOD! Let God orchestrate your life as he sees fit. His will for your life is best for you. Nothing is better than being in his perfect will. Trust and believe!

SELF DISCOVERY

Make a list of ten things that you will now trust God for.
God I trust you for…

_____

_____

_____

_____

_____

_____

_____

_____

_____

_____

_____

Every morning, add this to your affirmations. God, I
Trust you!

DAY 27

REMEMBER GOD'S PROMISES

God's promises are what you need to explore and visit on a daily basis. How else will you know that God can take care of you if you do not read or know his word? Pick up the Bible today and read a few verses. Make it a habit of reading some of the word every day. Put a Bible App on your phone and read books that help you understand the Bible better. Search out scriptures that will help you in life's situations and watch how you navigate through life better.

God's promises keep you renewed, recharged and refueled. Grateful Life Creations pillows are here to remind you of God's promises. I needed to surround myself with positivity and constant reminders of God's promises in addition to reading the Bible. Placing God's promises on pillows inspires me daily, it can bring God's promises to light for you too.

SELF DISCOVERY

What are your favorite three scriptures and why?

_____

_____

_____

_____

_____

_____

_____

_____

_____

_____

_____

_____

_____

_____

_____

_____

_____

God's promises remind you of his never ending love.
Keep standing on his promises

DAY 28

GOD ROCKS

God is the best thing that has happened to me and you too. Just where would you be without your awesome God? He is always available and blessing you. He heals, he loves, he gives, he saves, he provides, he guides, he defends, he protects and he forgives.

God is amazing, and he wants you to know you are amazing, too. He made you in his image, and he loves you so much!

SELF DISCOVERY

As a reflection of an amazing God, how do you rock?

_____

_____

_____

_____

_____

_____

_____

_____

Exalt God. He is worthy! God rocks!

DAY 29

REJOICE ALWAYS

"Rejoice in the Lord always; and again I say rejoce."
Philippians 4:4

Ultimately, you must rejoice always. God has been so good to you. He has given you chance after chance, mercy after mercy. God has always forgiven you and continues to give you a clean slate on a daily basis to do it better than the day before.

God's love is unfailing and unending.   He continues to rain down blessings in your life no matter what you have done. When you rejoice and lift up praises, God opens up the windows of heaven and showers you with his goodness. So you have a lot of reasons to rejoice. Show him your love by rejoicing always. Worship him, praise him and exalt him because God has been so good to you.

SELF DISCOVERY

Write down ten things you can rejoice about?

_____

_____

_____

_____

_____

_____

_____

_____

_____

_____

_____

_____

_____

_____

He is worthy of all the praise. Rejoice alone and rejoice with others...and again I say REJOICE!

DAY 30

LIFE IS BEAUTIFUL

"The Lord is my shepherd, I lack nothing. He makes me lie down in green pastures, he leads me beside quiet waters, he refreshes my soul. He guides me along the right paths for his name's sake." Psalms 23: 1-3

Your life is beautiful. All of the things in and around you make a beautiful masterpiece. Your beautiful life is colored with good and bad, highs and lows and twists and turns. When you learn to see your life through God's eyes you will recognize the true beauty.

Next, take a look around you at all of the beautiful things made by God. See the sky, trees, moon, sun, flowers, birds, oceans an even tiny butterflies as extensions of God's beauty. His beautiful handiwork also includes you. When you focus on the beauty within and the outside creations your viewpoint will change. Look around you, count your blessings and know that your life is beautiful. A grateful life is a beautiful life.

SELF DISCOVERY

"Finally, brothers and sisters, whatever is true, whatever is noble, whatever is right, whatever is pure, whatever is lovely, whatever is admirable—if anything is excellent or praiseworthy—think about such things."
Philippians 4:8 (NIV)

What makes your life beautiful? Where can you discover hidden beauty in your life?

_____

_____

_____

_____

_____

_____

_____

_____

_____

_____

_____

_____

_____

_____

"I know that there is nothing better for people than to be happy and to do good while they live. That each of

them may eat and drink, and find satisfaction in all their toil—this is the gift of God." Ecclesiastes 3:12-13 (NIV)

How will you be happy and "do good?"

_____

_____

_____

_____

_____

_____

_____

_____

_____

Keep your head up, Sis. Be uplifted and encouraged. Know who you are, love who you are, and live your life! It is your life, and God has a destiny for you. Do not give up. Make it to the finish line with everything you have within. Keep moving, keep pushing, and keep pressing. Things will be good, then bad, then good again, but that is life. Life is still beautiful and so are you.

Be encouraged and be grateful because Sis, YOU ARE AMAZING!

A Final Thought

Sis, thanks for spending your precious time with me these last 30 days. I hope you have been uplifted when you were down, enlightened where you needed clarity, and inspired where you needed some light.

Remember to work on knowing yourself, loving yourself, knowing God, and loving your beautiful life. Get excited about your future and be empowered by the inspiration around you.

God Loves you, and so do I. Grateful Life Creations pillows are here to inspire and remind you that SIS , YOU ARE AMAZING!

www.gratefullifecreations.com

www.ingramcontent.com/pod-product-compliance
Lightning Source LLC
Chambersburg PA
CBHW060158070426
42447CB00033B/2206